AF577134

A COMMON BOND

For Phebe,
with fond memories of
a delightful day "doing"
Delmas.
Kathleen
3/21/87

Happy Birthday, Eugene
February 20, 1976

A COMMON BOND

Poems

by

Kathleen Platt

221 Wood Street California, Pennsylvania 15419

FIRST EDITION of 2000 copies,
300 numbered and signed by the author.
This is No. 279

Manufactured in the United States of America

International Standard Book Number
ISBN 0-910042-28-4

Cover: *"Dense Gathering,"*
a watercolor painting (1975) by Bill Hanson
State College, Pennsylvania

Table of Contents

Preface

A Common Bond did not begin as a collection of poems linked to the women's liberation movement, nor is it, perhaps, an obvious product of feminist philosophy. Indeed, I hope that these forty poems will strike chords in men as well as women, and in women not drawn to Women's Lib. Still, the collection does have roots in a belief strengthened by this movement, i.e., that a woman judges life, and acts or reacts to its events from a perspective not shared by men, by her children, or even by all other women. Sometimes her judgments are painful, sometimes at odds with others' expectations. Sometimes they are bitter, and sometimes wry. As we are beginning to recognize, however, they are not isolated and not invalid.

For the most part, *A Common Bond* commemorates a group of shared experiences. Some of them were not obvious to those involved; some of them all too obvious. Some are shared with more people than I guessed when writing them. I am most grateful to those who let me learn that we do need to know about each other, about the links and the common bonds among us all.

I would like to thank the editors of the following publications in which several of these poems first appeared: *The American Magazine, Bitterroot, The Blackbird Circle, The Cardinal Poetry Quarterly, Caryatid, Gryphon, Hibernia* (Ireland), *Liaison* (Ireland), *Monument, The Paper, The Pembroke Magazine, Pocket Poetry, Poem, Sand Castles, The South Carolina Review, Voices International, Wind.*

Kathleen Platt
February, 1976

WOMAN AND MAN

Lifesong

We two are migrant seekers,
never home.
We have touched down
in a dozen runaway places
of the world,
stopping midflight to find —
to tie the knots we need
and soon will slip away from.

My body aches
if I am still too long,
sedentary in a single pose,
  a too familiar place.
I have not gathered yet
the flowers and the fruits
sown wild for me,
nor finished for those who will follow.

When we pause,
my woman's heart sends out feelers
like an ivy rooting in water.
They find and tangle in harmonious growth
from other fast or floating spirits.

When we move again,
I tear myself away,
glad of the new horizon,
  bright with expectation.
Yet all of me does not fly.

Sometimes
I try to take along the treasure
of my old world,
but it is heavy baggage,
and slowly falls away.

It seems the simpler thing
to leave a bit of my bone,
my blood behind.
My eyes are often absent,
looking at an old landscape.
Occasionally I am short of breath,
cooling the porridge
set before my children, long ago.
There is even a bit of me left
tending the garden where you found me,
plucked me from the green bush,
and set my stem to water.

Cold Comfort

The snow,
everlastingly constant,
drifts through every Pennsylvania day now.

While you were gone
it settled on top of the ground we knew
and kept it still,
but filled the space between us, too,
and kept us from touching.

Now that you have walked out of the flurries,
no longer lost to view,
the snow covers the days that passed between us,
keeping them still.

Our Separate Ways

You, flying again over the ocean
that rift and righted us
closer than before;
waves from my side built
and rocked your shores then, and they,
returning, bearing American melody,
splashed loudly in the places I kept empty
for your return.
As I wait this time,
as it begins again,
the ledger fills with longings,
my dreaming embrace a half circle,
unfilled by the form it is bent to hold;
still you fly on, reeling out our magic,
an elastic thread that tenses as the miles,
now hours and soon days and darkness
interpose their weights,
storing energies that will propel us
one into the other
when at last your direction is reversed.

Our movements are so cyclic,
some of them begun, ended in a day,
others of unconscious pattern,
leaving us to wonder at the final arc
bearing still the rhythm and the even measures
we have wrought and then forgotten.

We, like the tides between us
travel from one depth to another,
play out our energies
and then rebuild.

Again you are gone
and I who long for more hours
in each day
that I may more often exercise my grand intentions
and my simpler joys

find that these things have no bulk
without the backing you lend;
still, I do them now,
disciplined against the waste
of hours and energies.

I feel my body gathering,
the tenderness in my breasts,
I bend with the commotion of my womb,
unable to manage words.
How strange it seems that this,
a monthly feature of our common life
should continue in your absence.
To find that my body works without you
is like the shock of coming apart
from utter union,
yet this is how it must begin,
continue, and one day end.

We witnessed life and death today,
birth in the field beside the station,
the gentle but insistent murmurs of a cow,
tossing her head from the tall grass
as the farmer pulled
and fell and pulled again and still again,
stretching the legs of the darkling form
into a line — surely the bones will snap,
the sockets lose their grip —
another moan, and then,
a calf lying separate from the mother
who stands, empties the waters of her struggle,
and turns, ready in her new role;
death brought close from another coast,
plane down and shown in flames,
not yours,
thank god we haven't entered that one in our book
that grows as we come and go
together and apart
and back together.

A Test of Talisman

Even as the first few miles
fall between us
small and separate fears
lay seige to my heart;
the shadows of clouds passing the window
move among my thoughts,
cold,
disquieting,
the color and shape of premonition.

I am trespassing here,
for we are heavy creatures of the earth,
my unborn child and I,
and do not take so easily
to shifts of altitude and speed,
sending us after our prayers,
taking us where dreams alone
can float without encumbrance.

I am trespassing here,
clinging to the charm of superstition,
a metal talisman
whose weight and meaning
are earthly properties,
a link with slowly rooted things.

Will these wings that kept you safe
through a thousand dizzy leaps
down,
   down,
through the nesting games of sparrows
and the sober search of larger birds for carrion,
these wings now pinned above my heart,
will they remember
and return me too?

Fireside

At last
there are no miles between us,
no space of more than inches;
together by the gleaming ash,
we are close enough to touch
   or talk
      or love.
You are barely visible
in the glow of cinders,
shifting and tumbling with a sudden burst of sparks
like our thoughts,
and yet, though we are joined by this moment,
there is the memory of long nights, and
separate hearths, and unrelenting sorrows
which will divide us for a time to come.
Even if we burned a new log every night
the forest would long be around us.

Home

Her perfume mixes
in the thick slush of lather
from your palms,
white bubbles covering arms, shoulders, neck,
curling with the darkened blond
of your chest,
traveling quickly through the gullies of arched back
and sliding down your body
in smooth surrender
as the shower hits.

Steam rises,
a fog that still separates
you from my reality;
the weekend circles your feet
and then is drawn by the drain.
In my own fog of uncertainty,
I am listening to the sounds
of reclamation,
wondering what skin
will move out of this mist,
blood rising
from the brisk towel rubbing,
touching all the places
you have been together,
and we
before you went away.
My own flesh is strange
beneath clean sheets,
old blankets.
Both its impulse and its hesitation
worry me.

Morning Prayer

Waiting for daybreak
wrapped in shy, remembered ecstasy
and wistful in renewed desire;
stretched along a curve from hope
to fear,
knowing in the early minutes after sleep
that my heart may chill
when sunlight warms your face
and ends your dreaming reverie.

Will you remember who I am
and will you smile?

False Dawn

A gentle kiss
a soft caress . . .
it might have ended there
   with beauty
and then a nerve was touched
and we were fierce.

The cries, the clocks of another world
came between us;
we parted
and I walked without you,
body warmed from inside out,
glowing with your gift.

Moments

Later, this will be a memory,
lying here together in our first bedroom,
watching the moon dim
and burn to brightness again
in the narrow corridor of night
between the houses.

This conversation of being near
would be destroyed by words
   even whispered,
thundering, sundering
moon and mood.

Decision

Eight days . . . nights, then,
loving
    needing,
wearied by the struggle to turn from knowing
    what together would be;
longing to find a braille for your blindness,
and instead, discerning your discomfort
    among foreign hopes,
        strange dreams.
Feeling the cutting edge of adage
    that life's best things are free
        or freely given,
and turning from that other, treasured fiction
        to let you go.

A Love Ago

One day you came
to that vast Federal catacomb
where I spent my days,
and searched among the endless cells
until you found the doorway
that watched my desk.

You stood how long lost in grief
that we had shed our months of gay abandon.

Under the weight of your watch
I rose
and traveled the tunnel of your gaze

. . . but it was
as to a memory.

We were merely drifting together,
storing a temporary warmth.

December Fare

Loving you,
I am a winter bird,
derelict from the wisdom
of my species,
   long gone south
   where food and warmth abound,
   the darkness there a gentle friend
   of tired wings.

I fly in the empty spaces
left by fallen leaves.
Sometimes I reach
for a restful perch
and find that there is ice
within my grasp.

There is no food that grows
nor warmth that waits
within the winter forest.
I stay
to greet the child
who brings me daily
crumbs of holiday cake
and offers me
the brief shelter of his love.

Each night the earth turns
from the distant promise of December sun
and the child returns home.

Quickly the ice tips my wings
and I must fly in the darkness
to stay alive.

Each new day
I wonder
if the child will come.

Looking for Joe

In the men I meet
and the men I love
always I look for one.

Always I listen for words
he would have spoken
had he stayed
or had I stayed somehow
uncomplicated, untouched by my reality.

With a tall man
I lean again into his shoulder
holding dear a moment of false peace
and counterfeit joy.

I walk even into the minds
of those I love,
seeking his ideas,
gentle with his error.

Woman Thinking

Yes, women think of their men
when the men are gone.
They gather words spoken
in earlier hours
and turn them over and over.
They steady fleeting glances.
They treasure.

> We talk above the children,
> who punctuate, you say.
> Still, I easily separate your words from theirs,
> place them as I think you meant them to fall,
> hear them in your voice.

Woman, thinking of man,
becomes his.

Echoes

Do you come here too
on trips from the world
  we couldn't share?

Do you come
  alone now
and do you still say
  "champagne."

Here among Chicago's Seven Continents
do you travel that other?
  Elusive,
    ephemeral,
      remembered.

Does your gaze wander
  savoring the far corners yet unexplored
where it is still possible to find more
  than a memory?

That sudden someday meeting again
will it be here?
Will there be champagne
  and tears?

Reaching Out

You stand at the window, waving.
Another hour, you would as calmly open it in stealth,
give me a hand up or down, hold the ladder steady
for ascent or descent, exit or return,
stand as my shield.
The keeper, sending his bees forth to the world
to gather the sweetness of strange flowers,
also keeps the hive in order for their return.

Curious about the culture of happiness,
its properties like yeast— expanding, doubling in bulk
when allowed to mix with foreign mediums,
you try to find the ideal combination
of privacy and privilege, warmth and fresh air
for the perfect maturation of our marriage bread.

Spurred to recapture the hot color of the first flowerings
in our now well-cultivated garden,
desiring a spider who freely spins her webs and wonders
to play in the tangled growth of your own grasses,
you seek organic richness for our soil.

The backroads miles are thick with memories,
counted by steady revolutions, black on white,
slowing often for the small towns that link the farms and mines
of Pennsylvania
with the markets of her sister states.

The freshly painted fences of upstate New York
mark the halfway point in this journey into the past
for the sake of a future less known to us
than to those who follow the patterns of generations
and keep only a homefire burning.
Soon to be owned briefly
by a form inseparable from the hopes and fantasies
and sweetbitter love of younger days;
held again as the slender child of light
in the grip of that despair that time has let me understand.

The revolutions cease.
I smile at the demons of our past
rushing out of the ether
as the poles of our separate lives are brought again
into one room . . .
they are friendly folk,
each one a caricature of some recollection.
Shaking off the attic dust
that dims those treasures put aside
but not sold into uncaring hands,
they poke at this strangely present moment,
stretching, coloring it,
until your soul escapes,
leaps into the space that we must keep a moment longer,
giving reality a chance to dissipate in daydream,
or in the mystery of midnight sensation,
born of a freakish slumber, tangible and tantalizing . . .

Simultaneously the sounds of greeting
and the temperature of new embrace, old embrace
span the months, years of separation.
Remembering youth we grow back,
and shyly, too, returns the longing
for moments when all senses will be paired
and met and multiplied.

Much later, with demons laid to rest,
and long, telepathic thoughts bridging the miles
and other gaps in conversation,
I will return to liberation,
and you to your restrictions;
yet briefly, neither lives for us
who have one room, or two
with a soft light for blending unforgotten days
and nights
with this curious present
and its unguessed possibilities.

The Heart of Charlotte Amalie

We awake to the peace of an island morning;
your body, a shade warmer than the air,
settles against me.
The clatter of palm fronds
sifts through the high, narrow shutters,
just ahead of the deep tolling of a bell.
Slowly the timbre of human traffic scales the heights,
the rum browned sounds of night life are stilled,
and with them the small wraths and hatreds
we brought to bed.
In the freshness of a new day
we awake to joy.

A Dialectic

It is never a clean wound,
but a jagged line of flesh,
snaring memories, holding fragments
of the memories, so recently bright.

Why are the thirties
so destructive?
The reach of the scythe
so broad?

It would seem a time
for mitering the corners of a life,
turning from one half to another,
a settling, a synthesis.

And yet we tear at each other,
fighting familiars
in the face of strange fears.
It is not really you
who are the enemy,
but you are close.
My hand has learned the soft and hurtful places
of your skull,
and of the other,
the distant one,
I do not know what places there
are safe to pierce and turn away.
These days are sharp, and narrow.
They slit the seam of thirty years,
slicing careful cloth into fragments,
pieces needing pattern again.

Because of this destruction,
this unpiecing,
my poems do not form in lines,
in phrases typed upon a shining page;
they fall into prose;
they are letters and long distance calls;
they are hope and fear and love and hate
seeking some new alchemical bond.

Ode to a Most Unscientific Farmer

Daily I grow fuller
with the fruit of our union
upon reunion.
I am round, and ripening;
my cheeks appled even by winter sun, yet
I am no more an apple,
crisp and firm to your bite;
my flesh, my juices have mellowed,
softened with the pear sweet history of your touches
plumbing my depths,
sounding the strength of my tissues,
testing the bed from which your seed
will spring to manhood.

I hold this seed beneath the warm
white layers of my flesh,
the summer's glow still golden on my skin,
the promises of spring already stirring
in the fullness of my changing shape.
The simple seed has long since shed
the confines of its single cell,
has joined the medley of my own genes
and is exploding into theme and variations.
Together you and I have felt the pulsing rhythms
that yet escape our ears.

Our children all sleep warm tonight:
one at peace in a darkened room,
secure beneath the comforts of an eiderdown;
one bedded down inside a cavern
of mysteries without fear,
piecing together the substance of a new life;
the others wait
in the darkness we have not yet dreamed in,

and out of which will come
the stranger loves
to fill the spaces waiting
in our mad mosaic of todays,
yesterdays, and tomorrows.

Aren't we always
putting together the pieces,
not that our design is often shattered,
but like deciduous legions
we are seasoned by the passage of time,
we give up our greenness,
and leave some parts of our beginning behind.
Some of them fall upon our children;
they form a pungent mulch
from which the new life must extract
the lessons of survival.
They leave us free
to push new shapes and colors
into the light of day
and the uncertainty of night.

Tomorrow my body will bear cherries,
small and blushing crimson,
their succulence unequalled
by commercial formulas.
The honey of my mothering
will bring forth melons,
easily bruised and tender
to your touch.
There will be days
when the bitter oils of a rough exterior
enclose the sweetness that you seek;
then you must find still gentler words
for my affection.

You come and go,
sometimes peopling my world,
sometimes withdrawing
into your own resources.
When you are gone I miss you,
all the while knowing
that the contours of our garden
are not fenced,
and that they wander far
beyond the shade and solace
of a single tree.

Like a milkweed pod
your winged seeds may fly with the wind,
and come to rest in unpredicted furrows,
and some of them may send forth healthy sons,
sons that will fly on white, spidery wings
whispering of fleeting beauties.
Beauty whispers
in our own mating seasons,
falls softly with a strand of my hair
brushed between your fingers,
springs lightly from the sense of your joy in mine,
dances wildly in the warm excitement of your summer dreams,
endures the winters of your hibernation.

WOMAN AND CHILD

New Worlds

How can it be that I,
stepping yet so imperfectly,
shall find the gentler course for you
and soon another?

Motherhood

This dream of Motherhood,
a nightmare.
I am heavy with the thought, the sound, the talk of it.
I want to stay and dream awhile,
spending away the currency of moonlight,
and dodging the copper glare of midday
which each day shows me larger than the last,
and still, that smooth uncompromising belly of time grows on.
Wretched worldly ruse,
casting me from my preserve
to do the will of species.
A child of ultimate embrace shall crawl between our kiss,
and inarticulate a stranger will.
O child, shown to me the second after birth,
still colored by the blood of our struggle together,
how shall I speak of love?

Biology for Smoke-Filled Rooms

The male scent of cherry embers
from a dozen scattered pipes
fills the heavy silence
of a hundred listening conferees,
their chairs scraping occasional pockets in the hush,
their bones impatient at the discipline
of lengthy speeches;
the vocal point of concentration tires,
trails on,
forgetting the relief of inflection,
pursuing the end arranged in earlier hours;
the will to follow his words,
to anticipate his direction
contorts my features, constricts my posture
for long moments
until the world held privately within me
protests its own impatience
to know the end of darkness,
protests the confines of my brittle pose,
kicks out in random pattern,
shattering my concentration,
and drawing my thoughts inward.
To the new life restless in my womb,
I will one day try to justify the strictures I impose;
briefly, I am glad to have them broken,
to feel the duality of my own existence
ripening.

Phantoms (for Paul)

A small white horse
keeps its breathless pose,
eerie and surreal
as the earth bends into twilight,
as evening turns its face;

the white horse shimmers
as the ghoul of after hours
stares into the stillness of the yard.

It waits so
in the early mist;
it is calm in the heat of midday.

Then, in a seeming blur,
a tumult of eager, unschooled limbs,
of childish melody,
the horse moves —
but for a moment.

Headline

HEADLINE:
We are the children of Biafra.
By August we will be dead.

I, a child of fortune.
A dollar a week for making my bed.
An allowance for my prodigious needs.

It never occurred to me
to wish for sunshine,
for a day,
for September.

There are, too, the children of Harlem,
  Watts,
    and Washington.
Today, tomorrow, or
  by August . . .

Carlos

On the last day
the bag broke.

It was a ritual act
each evening at dusk.
The loneliness of his eleven years
spilling out into the street
recently emptied of younger children,
his large sneakered feet dragging
with his spirits
and the plastic wrapped garbage of the day.

The scraps, garnered
from the corners of several years,
swept from beneath the borrowed beds
and from the floors of closets this once uncluttered,
spewed onto the pavement
before the dumpster.
Its banging jaws, meant to devour
village discards and disappointments,
yawned futilely above the rubble.

This North American university town
was not his territory,
and the charm of his latin accent was lost
upon the residents of married students' housing.

He stirred the soggy paper trash,
the broken bits of bottles,
the cans and lids from jars
with his foot.
Mechanically, he scooped and stuffed
a few double handfuls into the bin —
foul and nearly full.

The oldest of the neighborhood children,
he played silly games with the smallest
to keep their company,
was first to learn the names
of babies and other new arrivals.
He was first
to seek the meaning of each new day,
brash with its birds, its blue sky,
sitting quietly at the swings,
trailing a stick in the sand,
waiting for the children of other families
to peal into the sunshine,
warm and full of morning oats
and early indoor fun.

There were so many empty jars of baby food,
plastic bottle liners and disposable diapers —
  the baby, fat and gurgling
  in the room they shared;
a stack of his mother's dissertation rough,
and the rolling, tinny echo of his father's thirst —
  a big man,
  auto mechanic by day, gruff by night.

There was little of the boy's past in the pile.
Little of him packed the day before
into the orange and silver van
that crossed the neighbors' yards at nightfall.

He sighed as he surveyed the remainder.
He stared at the neighborhood —
  the curtained squares beginning to glow,
  the metal swings melting into the shadows,
  the sand slipping away,
  the seesaw.

It rained
on the litter he left behind.

WOMAN ALONE

The Season

Today I bend over the raw earth,
deliberately torn, turned in upon itself,
I blend good soil with the worn,
crumble the rough geometry of nature
between my thumb and fingers,
spin the larger stones into a pile,
and let the smaller ones fall with the dirt,
holding space and air in the darkened mass
for earthworms, who will tunnel secretly.

When the soil is worked
and ready,
I spend my seed in careful patterns,
rows of shallow furrows
and a circle — for leeks.
They are my designs,
sometimes against the scripture
on the packet backs — "Thou shalt not
spill thy seed in April or in rows too close
to thy neighboring plants."

I do not know what strange and beautiful things
may grow in the wake of my license and my love,
only that the need to plant is strong,
and that the harvest of my creatures,
my own,
will loose some private joy
now locked beneath the layers of garden
and the slender shell of my seed.

Wanted

WAITRESS WANTED
for the hourly, half-hourly pattern
of unimaginative verbal caress,
  Hey, baby . . .
cigarette hanging
or careful in cupped shield,
Greek lettered signet gleaming
near the ash;
napkins with crude expressions
of erotic art,
empty matchbooks
bright with empty promise
of bigger biceps, breasts,
or bilingual ability;
the afterhours familiarity
heavy with the hand on shoulder,
waist,
forcing the flesh to tingle
in the second before revulsion
crawls along the short neck hairs
and down the spine . . .
a hand easy in its authority
before the day's accounts are settled.

A long chain of these jobs,
each one the last,
until in desperation
tired eyes seek and find again
the small white sign.

Fixing jaw,
sealing breasts against the wall
of cotton blouse
with one deeper breath,
pushing against the door
and met with yet another stare,
measuring, considering,
taking possession.

Summer, fall, winter.
One day
they found one of them,
hands stiffened in unnatural calm,
the flush of pursuit
darkening in a circle
on the floor.
Headlines, then,
WAITRESS WANTED.

The Trust

I am the long haired son of my father,
set to shoulder the weight of his world
grown too large;
I am the Legion soldier with hair
clumsy, furtive beneath beret,
not so that I might follow lover into camp and battle
but father through the future
that eludes him.

His true sons,
adrift in foreign disciplines, escape.
I, the first born, am less free.

The miracle of birth,
the cutting of a cord,
does not bring freedom to the child,
but ties him to the earth,
its people, its gravity.

For the parent, possessed briefly
of this simple, private power,
the gift of life is too precious
to be given freely, unrestricted.

It is I who must put my feet into the marks
pressed clearly in the sand of my father's time:
the careful legacy of a parent
mindful of his following.
I must feel the hot rough grains,
the cold night shade
that he has minutely remembered
for my inheritance.

Always,
someone must do these things,
else fatherhood rattle gracelessly
through the final years.

Needing Title

Without them,
the house is neutral, possible . . .
no territories staked out
by the warm breath of children,
fitting their fantasies between the walls,
the reach from floor to ceiling;
no body space
preempted.

I could shout
  HELP!RAPE!FUCKOFFMISTER!
—words my brain has pushed to the edge of my tongue
then rolled back between my tonsils.

I could dance upon the table.
I could stay out all night.
I could . . .

A black fly,
fattened over winter in the attic,
begins a hoarse stacatto
in the day's early brilliance.
His freedom, his life,
  his death are mine.

I kill him.

The Sun Lover

Scarcely anyone feels the April sunshine,
surprising the few who scuff at the water's edge
or rest akimbo, leaning into the shelter of boardwalk wall,
dreaming the winter darkened sand through pensive fingers.
Jeans flap and slacken with the wind.
Suddenly the pull of sunshine
on breasts too long confined by fleece and wools . . .
cautiously, then in abandon sweater pulled up
and elbows down, long hair catching
and combed by the ribbing;
the breeze circles and plays with newly surfaced flesh,
the sun continues to burn
his pride, his prowess.

Lying motionless, a stake in the struggle, perhaps conspiracy
between the elements,
again the hot pull of that power, that god of ancients
speaking without language to centers and sensations buried
beneath the channels of human conversation,
the message simpler, insistent.
Denim burning as through a magnifying glass
focused upon the second center of sensual comment,
setting molecules in motion that man with clumsy manipulation
may sometimes move and sometimes mot,
a bush of matted branches
imbued with its own heat,
a nest of warmth,
incubator of passions needing more now
than the male imagery of ancestral legend
and the machinations of mind seduced by the wayward season.

Flinging away the last constraints of clothing,
lifted into the hot, too hot embrace of that unseasonal sun,
hands and eyes closed, clenched,
one over the dampness sprung from interior heats,
one against the light that would deny a vision
of some dark shape,
strangely featured but sharing these rhythms,
working to complete the distance not yet disclosing
if he be cruel mirage or partner
to this impersonal greed.

Cultural Gap

I saw him low bending,
stooping, easy among the long damp furrows
with the feel of vegetables
in his hands.
I called to him,
soundless words
pulling from me, going
quite without me,
and I waited.

His sun wrinkled
crinkled face
soft brim shaded
from the glare of tableland
was a dusky shadow prism;
his steady eyes were full of resting,
unrelated to the acres of his life;
he seemed to see without looking
diesel people going by,
agitated, desperate . . .
I was one of these,
trying to forget
my star spangled truths
in time to listen . . .
just in time.

The Feminine Solution

Thirty years gone
along the trail to that almighty holy grail
I've been groping for
since infancy.

I marvel at the clues I've had
and failed to cipher:

at four
the trauma of seeing the sibling,
possessed of neat collapsible cork
where I was simply crevice,
looking from the fore
much like the aft
in minature;

perhaps a glimpse of father,
tossing aside a plastic curtain,
brought by hot water pricks
into full bloom,
all stamen (or is it pistle?)
like the fat brown cattails
that line the highways
in lusher states;

in seventh grade gym
when I was not issued
the private protection
sported by the junior males
(I needed the make believe bra
my mother bought
to demonstrate my sex
beyond understandable doubt).

Now it is all so simple.
I will begin my study
in September.
In seven years
I'll hang my shingle
with the rest of the foxy doctors.

My specialty will be the penis.
I will survey, observe,
test, treat, pinch, patch, pull,
incise, stitch, and catharize,
massage, measure, and ultimately
select the perfect penis for my own.

As a licensed practitioner
of medical arts,
my surgical removal
of the distressed organ
will be legal . . . perhaps hailed
as a major advance in the quest
for equality of the sexes.

I will care for it,
protect it well,
as I, of course, know how to do,
having been protected
many years myself . . .
perhaps under glass,
allowing no uncaste or foreign matter
to sully the sheen of its skin,
its violet complexion.

I would stroke it
now and then,
allowing it to swell
with the importance I give it,
but not to grow
beyond its proper bounds,
so that I could
no longer contain it.

Actually,
I think we'll be quite happy,
my pet,
my peeve,
my penis and me.

A Common Bond

Somewhere near Atlanta
you brush your hair
and break the furry skin of a Georgia peach;
you dress to go out at daylight
and tiredly climb the stars at night;
you wake to resume some unknown routine
with parts apart from my own
yet surely similar.

You call the name of a child
whose father is father to my own sweet child,
a man your son has never known
since that first begrudging permission.

Holding his son a few days after birth,
what store of father love,
what desperate messages of hope and pride
could he have sent beneath the blind
unseeing blue of infant eyes?
Was it enough to carry his child
through years of lawful separation
that binds the boy away from him,
holding the bond of mother-child more dear?

Now, as he holds his daughter
in the same strength of arm and heart,
I read the sometimes shadow in his smile.
I see him building perfect worlds for her,
a dewy paradise where she may gather friends
among wild flowers and gentle animals;
together they run in sunlit fields,
the gold of summer shining in their hair —
a shade that nature may have duplicated once before,
and their laughter finds an echo
in the hollow places of the woods,
and in the unhealed hollow of his heart
where once he held his son.

As I hold this man
and feel his tenderness overflow,
belying the strength of his limbs,
I think of his son, and wonder
if when you hold the boy
you ever think
of his father.

The Trip

Waking up with wonder,
the drug still funnelling
along the moon surface of my brain,
but the heavy traffic
of the eleven hour pain gone.

As the sun recedes
outside the even mesh
of wire and heavy glass,
the blindness
slowly leaves my mind.

Streetlights hang the night
on poles,
their sharp glitter
reminiscent of needles
into my subconscious
as I searched the drug for sleep.

My soul has gone out of this body again,
twisting into the night with a shriek,
and the dusky velvet
has moved in on me.

My new filler is restless too.
It races, slows,
paces my body, its cage.
It is a night fever,
escaping out of all my pores.
I am possessed strangely
by my strange possession.

I am tired,
eager for release.
The fever whispers black messages
behind my ears.
". . . the baby sleeping?"
". . . empty space in your marriage bed?"

What comfort lies with the weary husband,
sudden mother, father, keeper
of the make believe and
scary bedtime creatures?

Will that small part of the world
I move in
slow down a bit,
and let me climb back on
with the grace befitting a man
or woman
so recently come through seige?

Will I find my mind
out there somewhere
where I let it wander,
while the murky velvet spurred
my questions and concerns —

the right one, I mean,
that knows the codes
sent out by friends and family
for touching, listening, loving?

I hope to get out this time
without scrambling
the few memories that remain.

"In" Solution

Afflicted
with the cholera of melancholy,

I am here,
pulling the corners of me
into the core.

Next I will go in search
of my music
the dependable refuge
from a world too full
to hold its empty people.

The music varies,
a symphony,
a single flute searching for a ceiling,
a train calling into the darkness,
the ocean,
turning the sands,
tumbling the castles,
filling the tunnels of the day's children,
leaving the slate clean and vulnerable again.

I do ask
that my music come without words,
for I will pull it in after me
where there are words
in abundance waiting.

Windows

I am remembering the faces
of many men . . .
some of them seen from city buses,
their puzzled expressions unsolved
as the transit authority
kept to its own time and places;
one or two have pulled up
alongside of me . . .
   waiting for a signal.
Occasionally I have drunk their wine
and all too rarely
my heart has danced in their company.

From each of them
I learned
a part of what I need
to live with the loneliness
of loving.

Seasonal Preoccupation

Again October
brushes leaded glass,
leaves, tortured to one-time intensity,
giddy in the wake
of new velocity
that did not trouble
the green days.

I stand with heart touching the pain of autumn,
and hold the overbearing colors at bay,
a brief baroque
without the permanence of bleaker hues:

the unrelenting blue
and linear grey,
uncompromising backdrop
for compromise,
as we faced our own fall
on the out-of-season beach.

Elder Poet

Cornering a bit of weekly culture,
she is periodically animated, smiling
at faces familiar from other corners,
other bits and pieces
of brightly colored tragedies
turned to artful preoccupation.
She is eager, frightened, grey.
Most of her days have spent their rhyme,
and the young are desperate friends now.
The lines about her have all gone straight;
even the close cropped hair
severely combed
has lost its fibre with its sheen
and limply lies against her head.

Tonight I watched her hang
on the song of my words
and my own grey heart
went out to her.

Home is Where the Nurses

A year within the walls of your retirement,
the silences between us lengthen.
So much of your day dependent
on the strength of others,
you've forgotten the freedom of inquiry:
we must unlearn the courtesy
of two-way conversation.
Hesitant, we scrape our minds
for small details of every day's living.
It is not so much that there is less
to talk about
as that we fear contamination
of the good news:
tremble that the food we plan for tomorrow's fete
will reek of antiseptic;
worry that this dry arrangement of wrinkled flesh
will pinch the cheeks of children,
fading now in frames
beneath the white reflected sun;
clap our hands against our heads,
knowing that the calls, the cries of these halls
will invade the castles at the beach
again this summer.

You wake and sleep in tandem
with a dozen feeble neighbors;
you nod before the glare of television,
impervious to the sound — gone or blaring,
the colors garishly awry;
someone feeds you too,
at measured intervals,
relieving you of the puzzle of your hunger.

The motherhood that is upon me
shrinks from the certainty of this fate,
too late, the children borne,
growing into their early days
that have become the high noon
of my bloom.

Grateful, fearful of our remaining differences,
we resent your disabilities,
we weary of the bitterness
that attends your closing hours;
our visits are briefer,
less frequent.
And yet we do not escape.
When you are lost in thought
the clatter of your needles is terrible,
knitting together your wounded memories.

Symbols

Flowers sent
to welcome a child,
to color the joy of new beginnings,
to lighten a mother's memory of struggle
shared by green and ripened limbs,
spring into a winter colored world,
dominate the antiseptic decor,
recede when child is brought to bed,
become the child when he is gone.

Flowers tendered
to win first love,
to sweeten the suit of raw hungers,
to speak the words still awkward
on tongue more used to whistle than to woo,
proclaim a victory, worn with inborn blush,
imply a pact of warm and musky odors,
begin a ritual search for pleasure,
become the love surrendered.

Flowers laid
to stay the moment of final truth,
to cover flesh bereft of inner bloom,
to warm the chill of thin fingered death,
lay down their own sweet lives,
stretch severed stems toward the soil,
wither
and become the dead.